Georg Kugler

Franz Joseph & Elisabeth

History of a fairy tale couple

Pichler Verlag

AUSTRIA-HUNGARY, THE EMPIRE OF EMPEROR FRANZ JOSEPH

Thanks to the remarkable development of our mental capacity for reception since the Enlightenment in the 18th century, we Europeans, or those of us who have grown up in Europe, are in the position to envision culture from various regions and epochs. Many works of literature, music and above all applied arts from former centuries fascinate us, even though we hardly have anything more than a vague notion of the intellectual, religious and political power of the states in which they were able to develop – or judge them according to the foundations of our democratic and liberal nation-states in a smug way. For certain we don't want to have lived in these times and in any of these worlds. This also pertains to the great cultural centres in their heyday – to Rome of the 16th century, Holland of the 17th century and to Venice of the 18th century. We judge the moral conduct of the powerful, their religious intolerance or their political short-sightedness; admire without reserve, however, their artistic conviction or patronage. Our behaviour shows a divided relationship to the past. We should be critically questioning it and trying to comprehend the entire historical reality of the state or the epoch. We would soon realise that our criticism is premature, and our admiration superficial.

A historical state, which many encounter with huge political prejudices, but whose culture is simultaneously more and more admired, is the Austrian Empire or the Austro-Hungarian Monarchy of the second half of the 19th century, the empire of Emperor Franz Joseph.

However it is not only this empire that we critically judge today, but the whole self-confident and thought-to-be progressive nation-state of the 19th century – its exploitative colonial politics and its militant trade policy. The consequences thereof are the impoverishment of the Third World, the pauperisation of the large cities and the ruining of nature.

It wasn't the impoverishment of the working masses in the industrial society that was the main concern of the great powers of Western Europe – the impoverishment would have affected the powers themselves the most – but the question of nationality in other states. France and England, later also the United States of America, demanded a right of self-determination of all peoples based on the principal "Each nation one state, the whole nation only one state", and made their aim the suppression of both these rising multinational states – Austria-Hungary and the Ottoman empire. Disadvantaged for decades by a consistent foreign and trade policy, both these states were conquered and destroyed in the First World War. In 1918 the victorious powers constructed more than a dozen 'national' states, which all – even the brutally decimated Hungary – still remained

Above: Glamorous duel monarchy gala: the court ball. Aquarelle by Wilhelm Gause, 1900.
Opposite page: Banquet in the Great Gallery of Schönbrunn Palace at the 100-year anniversary celebration honouring the Maria Theresa medal. Painting by Fritz L'Allemand, 1857.
Page 2/3: Franz Joseph and Elisabeth (in the carriage) with the crown prince couple on an excursion in the Laxenburg Castle park. Painting by Carl Schweninger The Elder, 1887.
Page 6/7: Failed war hero: Franz Joseph at Solferino. Coloured lithograph, 1859.

multi-national or multireligious. The victorious powers weren't concerned about history, culture or religion, but with the dubious allocation according to language. The new states and mandated territory offered its people and ethnic groups neither security nor autonomy, which for example the Austro-Hungarian Monarchy had tried to offer them.

This complacent new nation-state of Central and Eastern Europe, which relied on the guarantees of the great powers, slid into civil wars and dictatorships, and finally two world wars. Without being attached to a larger whole, this nation-state was re-established in 1945 after the catastrophe of war. However it was only able to maintain itself with inhuman dictatorships, which pretended to solve the problems of nationality by the expelling, resettlement or murder of the people.

And yet, after half a century of dictatorship over these oppressed nations and religions, these states have failed again. The artificial state structure of the years 1918 and 1945 has collapsed. Slovakia became a republic in its own right, detaching itself from Czechoslovakia; the countries of Yugoslavia have become independent, divided roughly the way they existed as Habsburg crownlands. Italy had to reluctantly concede autonomy to the former Austrian regions South Tyrol and Friuli. Today the EU will be given the chance to adjust economically, culturally, religiously and on a national level.

With this goal in mind, our interest turns again to the history of Austria-Hungary, where in fact national conflicts ruled daily politics, which are still acute in many countries today. Here, however, unity of state and regionalism were able to maintain a balance until chauvinistic nationalism began to threaten the cohabitation of the ethnic groups and unsettled the belief of liberalism in law and reason.

Art and economy, to which the liberal upper classes had allocated its special attention and patronage, took on an unusual status during this epoch of political crisis, and due to their co-existence of multifaceted cultures and traditions, were not constricted but enriched. The traditional Austrian, Catholic culture of grace and sensuality, which was influenced by aristocracy until late into the 18th century, had its greatest achievements reflected in architecture, theatre and music. It was associated with the diverse, nationally defined artistic endeavours of the Hungarians, Poles, Czechs and Italians. A unique artistic atmosphere developed, and art became a part of public life, in which political actions either seemed futile or were considered abject. The heroes of the multinational realm were no longer politicians but actors, and musicians (and their critics), painters and sculptors, whose works decorated the numerous public and private buildings in the growing cities – mainly Budapest and Vienna. And they were scientists – above all the ones who admired the artists, namely the doctors. Groundbreaking innovations were accomplished in many areas of the sciences and medicine. Important philosophers and psychologists – coming from the medical sciences, such as Sigmund Freud – taught in Vienna and Prague. Art history was likewise justified as a university subject in Vienna, like many other 'modern' sciences.

Political movements, which were important for the whole of Europe, developed in Vienna – the democratic socialism of Viktor Adler, Theodor Herzl's Zionism, Bertha von Suttner's peace movement. Thanks to the effect of the great composers Brahms, Strauss, Bruckner and Mahler, Vienna became the centre of the musical world with a glittering opera and concert life. The masters of the so-called 'Viennese School', Schönberg, Berg, Webern and Krenek, prepared the radical break from tradition in the music of the 20th century.

Vienna, the hub of this intellectual life, however also experienced a huge economic boost through an important urban modernization during the reign of Emperor Franz Joseph. A monumental example of this development is the Ringstrasse. Its scope and the stylistic uniformity of its public and private buildings became characteristic of the epoch, in which not useful considerations but rather

Above: The *Monarchia Austriaca*, a conglomerate of countries and crowns: Maria Theresa's coat of arms, after 1765.

Opposite page: Corpus Christi procession on the Graben in Vienna. The emperor and his entourage in the 3rd row. In the centre, Crown Prince Rudolf flanked by body guards. Photo, ca. 1875.

cultural self-expression prevailed over the building process itself. But just prior to the finishing of the last grandiosities, namely both the court museums designed by Gottfried Semper in the 'Imperial forum', the 'Ringstrasse style' became the object of hefty criticism, the symbolic point of attack of the sons for the epoch of their forefathers.

A new generation – like the new Vienna School of Music – was preparing a radical change, whose result, however, would put Vienna in the spotlight once more. Utilitarian and functionalist principles of city planning, humanistic ideals about new urban forms of life – for example social housing or democratic educational establishments – lay the foundations for modernity, just as classic as the paintings of Klimt and Kokoschka. Otto Wagner was able to realise large communal projects in the quickly growing city. His genius student Josef Hoffmann received European acknowledgement with his residential housing structures and villas, as well as for his interior design, furniture and arts and crafts. Through its products the Wiener Werkstätte carried ideas throughout the world.

In Vienna, Prague and Budapest this epoch of poets and

writers, also columnists, played a remarkable public role. German literature can thank Vienna and Prague for several of its great masters: Hofmannsthal and Schnitzler, Kafka and Brod, Werfel and Zweig – and in Budapest, the great metropolis of Austria-Hungary – Hungarian literature contributed substantially to the self-confidence of the city. This world that vacillated between dream and reality, between aestheticism and materialism, found its admonitory conscience through Karl Kraus, publisher of the newspaper *Fackel*.

Emperor Franz Joseph supported this development more out of a sense of duty than out of conviction. Ultimately, he judged himself and the multi-ethnic state as an anomaly. But this was a time-bound judgement. Fifty years later, the great Austro-American historian Robert A. Kann evaluated this state very differently: "At the time the political history of the Habsburg Empire was ending, its cultural message to the world was just beginning".

Yet today we can see what an important role a head of state who is independent of daily politics played as an integral power. Franz Joseph, Emperor of Austria, King of Hungary and Bohemia, appears today, again, as he did 100 years ago, as a symbol of an ethnically encompassing state idea. Finding out more about him, about his weaknesses and strengths and his failures, is the goal of this book. It is dedicated to him and his beloved and beautiful wife Elisabeth – a cult figure during her time and also today.

Franz Joseph descended from one of the oldest European dynasties. His ancestors had been emperors of the Roman Empire since the late-Middle Ages and German kings until the great central European realm was destroyed by the imperialism of Napoleon.

Since the 13th century the Habsburgs had been dukes of Austria and Styria, expanded their sphere of influence southward as far as the Adriatic Sea, westward to the Rhine, and affiliated with the Netherlands through the marriage of Maximilian I to Maria of Burgundy.

The blossoming French-German culture of this rich and powerful complex of territories influenced many generations of the Habsburg family. Even today the Order of the Golden Fleece (*Toison d'or*) is a reminder of these cultural bridges between Brussels and Vienna. From Burgundy the Habsburgs connected with the Spanish ruling families, from Vienna, with the ruling families of Bohemia, Moravia and Hungary. Maximilian's grandson Charles V, born in Gent, led the Habsburgs to world power. In the 16th century the 'House of Austria' was divided into a Spanish and German line. In 1736, Maria Theresa, daughter of the last Habsburg emperor Charles VI, married

Above: The emperor visiting the Crownland Galicia: Franz Joseph's reception at the train station in Lemberg. Painting by Antoni Kozakiewicz, 1881.

Opposite page: Eucharist Congress, Vienna, 1912: entrance of the papal legate Van Rossum and Emperor Franz Joseph with heir to the throne Franz Ferdinand on Heldenplatz. Painting by Alexander Pawlowitz.

Duke Franz Stephan of Lorraine, who followed his father-in-law as Emperor Franz I. Since then, the dynasty has been known as that of Habsburg-Lorraine.

Following the end of Napoleon's empire, the old empire was not reconstituted, and the Habsburg crown-lands were combined under the collective name 'Austrian Empire'. Each of the countries, however, carried its historical title. The Emperor of Austria was King of Bohemia, Dalmatia, Croatia, Slavonia, Galicia, Lodomeria and Illyria. He was Archduke of Austria and carried the title of Duke of Styria, Salzburg, Carinthia, Carniola and the Bukovina. He was Grand Prince of Transylvania, Margrave of Moravia, Duke of Selesia, Friuli, Ragusa and Zara. Alongside Austria, he also reigned over the country complex of Hungary, which was likewise as large, as Apostolic King of Hungary.

Elisabeth's great-grandfather, Duke Wilhelm of Birkenfeld-Gelnhausen in the Palatinate, married a sister of Prince-Elect Max Joseph of Bavaria, who gave him the title 'Duke in Bavaria' in 1765. Elisabeth's father, Duke Max, married the Bavarian princess; her older sister Sophie married Archduke Franz Karl of Austria: her oldest son was Franz Joseph.

The future marriage partners, then, were cousins. Their joint life had a fairy tale beginning, but ran unhappily and ended tragically. Elisabeth was an imaginative, artistically talented child of nature who couldn't reconcile herself with the official and political duties as Empress of Austria. The life alongside the military-educated and duty conscious Franz Joseph, who was considerate to be sure, but unimaginative, and who was absolutely absorbed in his governing responsibilities, appeared to be unbearable. She fled the court, spent many years of her life travelling, although she loved her family. The beauty of her appearance, but also her personal sympathy for the fate of many people, particularly her sympathy for the Hungarians, won her admiration and adoration which is still valid today.

FERDINAND MAX. FRANZ JOSEPH. CARL LUDWIG.

ERZHERZOGE VON OESTERREICH.

CHILDHOOD AND YOUTH OF THE RULING COUPLE

When the engagement of the young Emperor Franz Joseph to the Princess Elisabeth 'in Bavaria' was announced on August 19, 1853, in Ischl, it was a sensation – for nobody knew the bride and hardly anyone knew about this princely family, which descended from the Count Palatine of Birkenfeld-Gelnhausen. Elisabeth was barely 15 years old and was called 'Sissi'. As mentioned, she was a cousin of the bridegroom, because their mothers were sisters, princesses of the Bavarian royal house. So Elisabeth's uncle was King Maximillian II of Bavaria. Sissi was completely surprised by the situation – even confused – because both mothers' plans were meant for Sissi's older sister Helene. A family meeting in Munich was to initiate the young emperor's happiness in life, and the Bavarians' visit to Ischl was to bring the desired result.

Elisabeth had had an easy-going and very happy youth, partly in Munich, partly in Possenhofen at Starnberg Lake. Her family was dominated by her mother, who came from Wittelsbach, while her father Max, a restless, fun-loving, sometimes almost whimsical man, was constantly travelling and left the upbringing of his many children to his wife. When he was present, however, he entertained young and old with singing and by playing the zither; he played with the children in the park, preferably at the Starnberg Lake, for he loved nature. In this way Elisabeth took after him, and would roam the landscape surrounding the lake, which was still largely unsettled. Her love of mostly sentimental or trivial poems also seems to be based on impressions from her childhood. She was a very young, yet unformed but open person – but at the same time a spoiled young woman, who had to consolidate her character, deepen her knowledge and collect experience under very different, unforeseeable, living conditions. Of the living circumstances of the thousands of people she would encounter in the next few years in the huge multinational states of Austria she had no idea. She reacted as often with sentimental concern as she did with deprecating apathy. And even in her youth she fled reality into a world of make-believe, which she let her husband pay for.

Franz Joseph had an entirely different childhood and youth. When he was born on August 18, 1830, in Schönbrunn Castle and was christened the next day with the names of three emperors – Franz Joseph Karl – no-one thought that he would ever be called on to rule. His father, Archduke Franz Karl, was the younger son of the reigning Emperor Franz I of Austria and brother of the heir to the throne Ferdinand. Many thought the latter to be unfit to rule but nobody dared to make any decisions for the future. Perhaps it was Franz Joseph's mother, Archduchess Sophie, who thought of a responsible and maybe fate-filled future for her new-born, for she was realistic and ambitious. In any case, Emperor Franz became godfather of his first 'Habsburgian' grandchild. The emperor resided in the

Above: An imaginative, artistically talented child of nature: Elisabeth, the young empress. Coloured lithograph by Eduard Emperor based on a painting by Franz Schrotzberg, 1856.
Opposite page: Franz Joseph with his siblings Ferdinand Maximilian and Maria Anna Karolina. Lithograph by Josef Kriehuber, ca. 1837.

Vienna Hofburg, preferably stayed at Laxenburg Castle with its English park or the emperor house on Stadtplatz in the bourgeois health resort of Baden.
Archduke Franz Karl on the other hand preferred the Baroque holiday palace Schönbrunn, which Maria Theresa had once had redesigned as a family palace, and which played a certain role as venue for several parties during the Vienna Congress, but was otherwise mostly unused. The zoo, botanical garden and the park were, however, popular destinations for the Viennese. Its close vicinity to the people and the almost bourgeois-familiar atmosphere – in Hietzing far a field from the city, a place of pilgrimage, which some said was the most beautiful village in Germany of suited Franz Karl.
Emperor-to-be Franz Joseph didn't only spend most of his childhood there, but almost his whole life. And the family grew: in July 1832, Ferdinand Max, emperor-to-be of Mexico, was born; one year later Karl Ludwig, then a sister, Maria Anna, who died early, and finally in 1842 the fourth brother, Ludwig Victor.
The children didn't go to school but received intensive and strict private schooling in the fields of education that were then standard: religion, history, geography and languages. The military education began early and played a

large role. As a young boy Franz Joseph learned drills in infantry regiment 'Grand Masters of the Teutonic Knights', the Viennese house regime. At the age of 13 he became colonel of a dragoon regiment. His whole life long Franz Joseph preferred wearing a tunic as a form of clothing, and was a first-rate rider well into his later years.

While the reverberations of international incidences were hardly perceived by the eight-year-old Sissi, Franz Joseph, at 18 – also still very young – was experiencing war revolution. As in other European capital cities, a huge socio-political revolution had broken out in Vienna in March 1848, which challenged the cohesion of the Austrian multinational state and the existence of the Habsburg monarchy. Emperor Ferdinand 'the Benign', Emperor of Austria and King of Hungary, had to abdicate; the seemingly omnipotent state chancellor Count Metternich had to step down and flee.

Hungary strove to disengage itself from Austria to form an independent republic but, with the help of Russian troops, was quashed; the ringleaders of the patriotic uprising were executed, insofar as they were caught. The young poet Sandor Petöfi suffered a hero's death – in any case in the opinion of the Hungarians, and the nationalistic peoples' leader Lajos Kossuth fled abroad. For decades from Turin he condemned every attempt at political regulation.

The Italian population of the Habsburg kingdom 'Lombardy-Venice' – supported by France and England – also fought for disassociation from Austria, strove to unite with other Italian countries, and sought accession with the Kingdom of Italy. They all set their sights on the Savoyan Kingdom of Piedmont-Sardinia. Upper Italy became a battle field. Under the command of the aged field marshal Radetzky, who saved the state and existence of the dynasty, Franz Joseph experienced the baptism of fire in the battle of Santa Lucia.

And so Emperor Franz Joseph's reign began under inauspicious omens. Although the men of the foregoing epoch – the so-called 'Vormärz' (Pre-March Era) – were mainly responsible for the turbulent events, a dark cloud nevertheless hung over the accession to power of a young ruler, who was influenced by the spirit of an unfashionable absolutism. Not until years later, after several constitutional reforms, did he find a way to a constitutional state form – and thus to a liberal citizenship.

Below: An untroubled childhood: Possenhofen Castle on Starnberg Lake. Gouache, 1854.
Opposite page: The ambitious mother-in-law: Archduchess Sophie of Austria (1805–1872), daughter of King Maximilian I of Bavaria. Photo by Ludwig Angerer, 1868.

Photogr. v. Fr. Hohbach. Gedr. in J. B. Kuhn's lith. Anstalt. Lith. v. H. Kohler.

ELISABETH

Kaiserin von Oesterreich

ENGAGEMENT AND MARRIAGE

During the period before World War I, the marriage of their children was one of the most important concerns and an often difficult endeavour for parents of all classes. The great economic and social impact of marriage can be measured by this. In the ruling dynasties, parents not only took political considerations into account, but also turned particular attention to the worthiness of the marriage contenders. For their son Franz Joseph, who was appointed to rule, it was for this very reason his parents chose a woman who had to belong to a friendly European dynasty and furthermore had to be Catholic or prepared to convert to Catholicism.

The personally active and politically ambitious mother of the Emperor-to-be, Archduchess Sophie – who was said to be the "only man" in the Viennese court – planned a new connection between the Wittelsbach and Habsburg houses with her sister Ludovika. We already know that Ludovikas's eldest daughter Helene had been selected as the bride, but that Franz Joseph spontaneously decided on her younger sister, much to the surprise of the mothers. And because Franz Joseph stood his ground despite the resolute intervention of his mother, Ischl celebrated the engagement.

During the engagement year the bridal couple met both in Possenhofen, as well as in Ischl in the Salzkammergut, where Franz Joseph's parents spent their summer months each year. The small, idyllic town had really been a discovery. Archduchess Sophie attributed the happy birth of her son to the effects of the baths – which is why Archduke Franz Karl purchased a house in a rambling park, which became well known everywhere as the 'Kaiservilla' (Emperor Villa), and is a tourist attraction in Austria today.

Above: The fifteen-year-old Elisabeth. Photo by Alois Löcher, 1852/53.
Opposite page: Farewell to Possenhofen: portrait of the young empress with her homeland castle in the background. Lithograph by H. Kohler based on a photograph by Franz Hohlbach, 1853.

The seemingly happy engagement period was, however, an extremely difficult time for the young ruler and for the state that he wanted to rule, the Empire of Austria. After the defeat of the revolution, Franz Joseph paid homage to a neo-absolutism, in whose spirit the huge empire was to be centrally ruled through a loyal civil servant body and with the sole administrative language of German. The army, which had been ultimately victorious in 1848/49 remained threateningly at hand in the background as support for the system. And this is how the young emperor comprehended his chosen motto "viribus unitis" – with united forces. They were supposed to be united, the forces of all peoples, who, under his sceptre, were supposed to look up to him.

Those who had supported the national-political cause found this centralised system oppressive. Yet we shouldn't overlook that similar reaction to the events of the 1848 revolution occurred in many of the European states. In France the monarchy was dissolved and a republic was proclaimed. Louis Napoleon, a nephew of the great Corsican who was always admired in France, had himself elected as president of the republic in 1851 through parliament, and in the following year via referendum had himself elevated to Emperor. At the same time in the Kingdom of Piedmont-Sardinia, which continued to strive for unification with Italy with all its resources,

Camillo Cavour came to the top of the government as a strong figure. He was declared an enemy of the Catholic Habsburg ruling house, as was Count Otto of Bismarck, who, as the new authoritarian ruling chancellor of the strictly Lutheran Kingdom of Prussia, wanted to found a national German empire.

Initially a strong friendship joined the young Franz Joseph with the likewise authoritarian ruling Tsar Nicholas I of Russia. For the Hungarians – their country being the second-largest nation in the monarchy – this friendship was a thorn in their side as they remembered the Russian army's interventions in 1848, the year of the revolution.

Franz Joseph's round trip through the countries of the Hungarian Kingdom was supposed to dispel the resentment and win the hearts of Hungarians for their 'King'. Neverthless the situation continued to brew.

On February 18, 1853, the emperor was slightly injured during an assassination attempt by Hungarian János Libényi in Vienna. A neo-Gothic masterpiece by the archi-

Above: Numerous flyers announcing the engagement were distributed amongst the public.
Left: The solemn ceremony carried out by Archbishop Cardinal Rauscher in the Augustinerkirche April 24, 1854. Newspaper clipping from the *Neue Illustrierte Zeitung*, 1879.
Below: Elisabeth's bridal gown train. Kunsthistorisches Museum, Department of Court Uniforms.
Page 20/21: The bridal couple's outing on the day their engagement was announced, August 18, 1853, Bad Ischl. In the coach-box: Count Grünne, the emperor's general adjutant. Painting by Gottlieb Prestl from the Carriage Museum Schönbrunn, ca. 1855.

tect Heinrich von Ferstel, the Votivkirche, is a tribute to the fortunate outcome; the structure was a quasi upbeat to what would later be the Ringstrasse.

During the couple's engagement year Austria fell into an extremely unhappy position regarding foreign affairs. This was due to its futile intervention between Russia and Turkey in the countries' altercation about the so-called Danube principalities of Moldavia and Wallachia – from which later the Kingdom of Romania emerged. The so-called Crimean War broke out in 1854; and Austria, England and France fought at Turkey's side. Tsar Nicholas never forgave Franz Joseph for this course of action: Russia and Austria now found themselves in opposition in the Balkans, where their spheres of interest overlapped. Almost the entire Balkan Peninsula was under Turkish rule. Only Greece had become independent in 1830 with the warmest share of romantics in all European states, and until 1862 was ruled by King Otto I of Wittelsbach, a cousin of Elisabeth's and also Franz Joseph's.

Since the late 18th century, the Serbs, with the support of

Russia and Austria, had also achieved certain autonomy within the Ottoman Empire, whereas for the most part, both of the great powers supported different Serbian rulers. But the Serbs and Croats who lived under Turkish rule not only fought for their liberation but also for a coalition with those who lived in Austria-Hungary, for a mutual, independent state.
Neither the present nor the future of the state and its ruler could be described as assured, yet Franz Joseph was certain of his love for Elisabeth. The wedding date was set for April 24, 1854, naturally in the court church St. Augustin in Vienna.
Various portraits of the personable bridal couple and more or less sentimental paintings were painted and published; they were duplicated in Munich and Vienna. 'Sissi' quickly became popular both in her old and new home town, actually all over Germany and Austria.
Not much is known about her departure from Munich. A glamorous dress she wore to a farewell ball, for this reason called her 'wedding-eve dress', has been preserved. Otherwise, there are numerous paintings of her departure from Munich, the stops along the Danube on her journey on the paddle steamer 'Franz Joseph', her arrival in Nussdorf near Vienna, and finally her ceremonial entrance over the Vienna River into the city to Karlsplatz via the Elisabeth Bridge, which had been newly erected. These document the great interest the public and media had regarding this event – from which the reputation of the emperor could only benefit.
The solemn marriage ceremony, conducted by Archbishop of Vienna Cardinal Rauscher, was reported in a series of newspaper illustrations and lithographies based on fleeting drawings, which thus don't impart any convincing images of the huge celebration. The bridal dress was reproduced in a fashion magazine; the train has also been preserved.
The endless, solemn ceremonies, the huge number of people who searchingly examined her, were too much for Elisabeth. During her first reception as the new empress she broke down from exhaustion and left the room. A few days after the wedding she wrote the following lines:

Oh, that I had never left the path
That would have set me free
Oh, that on the broad streets
Of vanity I had never gone astray

From one day to the next, life completely changed for Elisabeth. From the small city of Munich, which under King Ludwig I had become a glittering *Residenzstadt* of cultural importance, and where art collections and artists stood in the spotlight, she came to the large, old Imperial City, still closed in by a moat and bastions, and where she could no longer move freely. The Hofburg was a huge, angular monstrosity that had been formed through the joining of various buildings, and was as old-fashioned as it was uncomfortably decorated. Sissi never liked being within its quarters; she associated even the most splendid rooms with the labours that public appearances and representation brought with them.
To begin with, the young couple fortunately moved to Schloss Laxenburg. But another, separate area of life that her sensitive soul was so in need of she was unable to conquer, and she had to renounce an undisturbed relationship with her husband: the emperor spent almost every day at the Hofburg, for in the first instance Franz Joseph was a ruler, then – son.
Indeed, Archduchess Sophie was the biggest hindrance for the personal and family oriented happiness of the young married couple. She was both Elisabeth's mother-in-law and aunt. As aunt she wanted to make her Bavarian niece Sissi a perfect empress; as mother she didn't want to renounce her commanding influence over Franz Joseph.
There wasn't much left for the two in the way of common things. They couldn't really indulge in their love of nature because each trip, each visit, was always a ceremonially regulated, representative ordeal. Sissi felt as though she was being politically used, presented, ogled and criticised. What remained for the couple was enthusiasm for horses and carriages, but here Elisabeth also had to first eke out many liberties against societal prejudices.
She obstinately followed her goals, sometimes also with-

Above: Elisabeth in a dress modelled on alpine traditional costume. Colour lithograph by Emile Desmaisons based on a painting by Franz Russ.
Opposite page: The bride. In Elisabeth's hand a miniature portrait of Franz Joseph. Painting, anonymous, ca. 1854.

Above: Elisabeth in the first year of marriage. Painting by Franz Schrotzberg, ca. 1855.
Opposite page: Franz Joseph as colonel of the Field Artillery Regiment No. 1. Lithograph by Eduard Kaiser, ca. 1855.

out regard to her close family, and distanced herself more and more from the scheming court society. Indeed, she became one of the best horseback riders of her time, not only riding *parforce* hunts at her husband's side, but also taking part in the most difficult steeplechases – a man's domain – in England as a woman.

Eduard Kaiser
nach der Natur gez:
GEDR. B. J. RAUH

PORTRAIT OF A MARRIAGE

The public knew and sensed nothing of the tension in the imperial court. Elisabeth and Franz Joseph were a beautiful couple; doubts about their personal happiness didn't seem to be indicated.

Their first child arrived in March 1855, that is, in the first year of marriage, a daughter, Sophie, who was hardly two years old when she died. In the following year, Elisabeth gave birth to her second daughter. She was baptized with the name Gisela – after Gisela of Bavaria, wife of Stephan I, patron saint and first King of Hungary. In August 1858, followed the birth of the much longed for crown prince, who was named after the first ancestor of the dynasty, the German King Rudolf I.

In the meantime, the political horizon had become somewhat brighter. The Crimean War had ended with the Treaty of Paris in March 1856. Yet the western powers were not thankful for Austria's fighting the war on their side. In the Italian Kingdom of Lombardy-Venetia, which was economically well developed, pacification and stabilisation was hoped for.

The southern railway line from Vienna had reached Venice in 1844 and its construction continued to Milan. Demonstrating confidence in this, the imperial couple embarked on a long journey through northern Italy in winter 1856/57. However the couple only received a lukewarm reception, which above all irritated Elisabeth. With the farewell of the residing elderly field marshal Radetzky in the same year and his death in the year 1858, an era came to a close.

As early as 1859, war broke out between Austria and Piedmont-Sardinia; under Emperor Napoleon III, France fought on their side. Bloody defeats of the Austrian army in the battles of Magenta and Solferino ended the century-long presence of the Habsburgs in Italy. At this point we are reminded that an epoch that had been as long as the Habsburg's reign came to an end: the most fruitful influence of Italian culture and art, not least in music. In the 17th and 18th century Vienna had become a partly Italian city. Builders, painters, craftspeople of all kinds, musicians and singers, poets and actors, officers and bankers, not least confectioners and chefs from all countries lived in Vienna. They served the emperor and many noble houses, designed and enriched the life of the city.

Austria naturally stayed connected with the world of the south. Still belonging to the realm were the eastern part of Venice, Trieste and its coast, which had been a Habsburg city for centuries, Istria and the Italian-Croatian Adriatic coast Ragusa (Dubrovnik) and Cattaro (Kotor).

Italy continued on its path towards state unification, but had to relinquish Savoy (the home of the new royal house) and the Riviera and ceded it to France. Napoleon III demanded his remuneration. Nice, Garibaldi's birth, city now belonged to France.

The time for decisive political reforms had arrived in Austria. The absolutist system was finally abandoned, and after two unsuccessful attempts, a constitution was established with the February Patent in 1861. At the opening of the Imperial Council (*Reichsrat*), despite concessions to

Above: Emperor Franz Joseph I in gala uniform. Photo, ca. 1855
Opposite page: No doubts about their personal happiness: Elisabeth and Franz Joseph as the Hungarian royal couple. Photo montage by Arthur Max based on photos by Emil Rabending, after 1888.

the crown lands, members of parliament from almost all nations opposed it: Hungarians, Croats, Italians, Czechs and Poles.

Following the birth of Crown Prince Rudolf, Elisabeth fell into an emotional crisis – not least evoked by her mother-in-law, who, in consideration of the empress' youth, formally seized the upbringing of the children. In his acquired veneration of his mother, Franz Joseph didn't manage to take up advocacy for his young wife.

Politics and court life were unbearable for Elisabeth; she felt estranged from her family, but Franz Joseph's long absences in the war year of 1859 were likewise as intolerable for her. Physically she was also at the end of her tether; she suffered from insomnia, inner disquiet and a chronic cough. In summer 1860 she fled to her paternal family in Possenhofen, and in late autumn, upon her doctor's recommendation, Elisabeth travelled to Madeira. Franz Joseph accompanied her to Bamberg. In Antwerp with a respectable entourage she boarded a yacht, which Queen Victoria had put at her disposal. For more than two years she travelled, equipped with the inexhaustible financing of the emperor, and only spent short periods in Vienna. So that she wouldn't lose contact with her children, the following year she secured a mutual trip of several months to Venice, which then still belonged to Austria, and subsequently a sojourn in Reichenau on the Rax. She didn't want to stay in Vienna. The time of Sissi's extended travels not only caused a caesura in her own life but also in Franz Joseph's. How little solidarity she thus showed him, how little feeling of responsibility towards the public, who experienced the military defeats and political changes with great dismay. Elisabeth returned to Vienna in August 1862, energetically admonished by her father Max. From then on she lived in the city for several years, her stays only interrupted by rejuvenating, summer sojourns in Bad Kissingen and Ischl, but a profound change had taken place. From the charming, melancholy young woman had emerged a self-assured, energetically demanding, and above all extraordinary beauty. Franz Joseph became her most glowing admirer, and she got everything she wanted. A traditional married life now no longer existed. In the legendary Ischl Ultimatum of August 1865 Elisabeth wrote, finally asserting her independence:

... that anything, which has to do with my personal affairs, such as the choice of my environment, the locality of my sojourns ... is reserved solely for me to dictate.

It was during these years that the representative portraits of the imperial couple were created by Franz Russ; also the disparately more impressive and today so famous works (which then seemed much too expensive to the emperor) by the German painter Franz Xaver, who travelled from Paris and was highly respected in all courts. The full-figure portraits – Elisabeth in a ball dress and with diamonds in her hair – and Franz Joseph in his marshal uniform, were meant for the presentation rooms in the castle; the more intimate, half-figure paintings of the empress would hang in the emperor's room until his death.

New political constellations had developed for the empire and the dynasty. The emperor's brother, Maximilian, the empress' favourite brother-in-law, allowed himself to be talked into accepting the crown of Mexico, and through it became a political tool for Napoleon III of France. In April 1864 he travelled from Miramare, his castle, which Elisabeth so loved, on the frigate Novara to Mexico – an undertaking that ended tragically: in June 1867 Emperor Max of Mexico was shot in Queretaro.

At the same time, Franz Joseph was attempting to enliven the German Confederation and sent out invitations for a German assembly of princes in Frankfurt. The idea was to find a new organisation for the German Kingdom, principalities and Hanseatic cities. A result was not accomplished for Bismark deterred King Wilhelm I of Prussia from attending.

Above: Extraordinary beauty: Elisabeth with open, flowing hair in robe de chambre. Copy by E. Riegele based on the original by Franz Xaver Winterhalter, 1864.

Opposite page: Franz Joseph's study in Schönbrunn Castle with the painting of Elisabeth by Franz Xaver Winterhalter from the year 1864. Photo by Raimund Stillfried von Rathenitz, ca. 1900.

Above: Soulful melancholy characterised Elisabeth's state of mind: photo taken late-autumn 1860 by Ludwig Angerer.
Opposite page: Elisabeth's living room and bedroom in her apartment in the Amalienburg.

The Prussian chancellor wanted to expel the multinational states of Austria from the German Confederation and force a national Germany under Prussia's leadership. As early as the year 1866 he found occasion to accomplish this goal through war. In the Battle of Königgrätz (North Bohemia) Austria was devastatingly defeated by Prussia and several cowardly affiliated German princes, and the German Confederation was dissolved.

Above: The imperial couple's bedroom in Schönbrunn Castle. The beds are made of priceless rosewood.
Above and below right: The representative pictures by Franz Xaver Winterhalter: Elisabeth in a ball dress with diamonds in her hair; Franz Joseph in Austrian field marshal's gala uniform wearing the Order of the Golden Fleece. Painting, 1864.

Above: Riding out together – a simulation. Photo montage on a correspondence card, ca. 1878.
Left: Franz Joseph and Elisabeth leaving the Badeschloss in Bad Gastein after visiting Emperor Wilhelm I. Photo by Max Balde, 1886.

Opposite page: A long-lasting relationship arranged by Elisabeth herself: Franz Joseph taking a walk with his 'lady friend', the court actress Katharina Schratt, in Bad Ischl. Photo, 1910.

Above: Lonely splendour in the Wienerwald: Elisabeth's bedroom in the Hermesvilla. The paintings on the wall illustrate Shakespeare's 'Mid-Summer Night's Dream', a work to which the empress felt particularly connected.

Above right: The Hermesvilla in the Lainz Tiergarten, commissioned by Franz Joseph and built between 1882 and 1886. It was originally conceived as 'Villa Waldesruh'.
Below right: Full-length statue of Sissi by Hermann Klotz at the entrance to her quarters in the Hofburg.

THE HUNGARIAN CORONATION

Winterhalter's paintings show Elisabeth at the height of her self-assuredness in 1865 – and for the first and only time in her life she became politically active. She was concerned about solving the problem of the smouldering Hungarian question. Since she had officially visited Hungary with the emperor for the first time in 1857, she had loved what her mother-in-law called the 'rebellious' country and its proud, spirited people, though she otherwise never showed feelings for her subjects. She gathered the Hungarians around her and began to learn their difficult language.

In January 1866 she was 28 years old when she met Count Gyula Andrássy, who as a Hungarian revolutionary had once been sentenced to death, in Vienna. As a result, the count invited the royal couple to Budapest in the name of the Hungarian nation, where they stayed for five weeks. Andrássy managed to use the queen as a political tool, and she was able to encourage the emperor and the king, who were so devoted to her, to accept negotiations between the Viennese government and Hungarian magnates. When, after the defeat of Königgrätz in 1866, the Prussians guarded the Lower Austrian border, Elisabeth fled to Buda with both children.

After a long game of tug of war, the negotiations were completed in spring 1867 and the 'compromise', which was often spoken about, between both 'halves' of the Habsburg Empire was achieved. Count Andrássy and Ferenc Deák, the actual creator of the contract, had reached their goal. From the Austrian Imperial State, which had existed since 1804 as a unitary state, the dual monarchy Austria-Hungary was formed. The common ruler of this empire now took the title 'Emperor of Austria, Apostolic King of Hungary', and each half of the empire was ruled by a prime minister. Working together were only the 'Ministry of Foreign Affairs and the Imperial House', the Ministry of War and the common Finance Ministry.

The glorious manifestation of this union – '*viribus unitis*' – was the coronation of Franz Joseph and Elisabeth to Apostolic King and Queen of Hungary. The ceremonies didn't take place in Pressburg – since the Turkish wars the traditional coronation city (Hungarian *Pozony*) – but in the city of Budapest, aspiring to be a city of one million people, which combined the royal city Buda, right of the Danube, and the business city Pest on the left bank of the Danube.

Similarly to Vienna, Pest above all had completely changed its face as a consequence of generous rebuilding. The parliament on the Danube, which catches every visitor's eye, was only able to become a large project after Hungary had been acknowledged as an independent government.

The coronation was held on June 8, 1867, in Matthias church on the castle hill of Buda. With this, the king guaranteed the ancient Hungarian constitution, which would well and truly exacerbate the exercising of his role as head of state. Elisabeth however, now the crowned and celebrated Queen of Hungary, had reached the highpoint of her life. The coronation was an incomparable medieval celebration, perhaps the last huge celebration of old

Above: Franz Joseph taking the oath to become King of Hungary (detail).

Opposite page: Still popular in Hungary today as *Erzsébet Királyné*: Elisabeth in Hungarian coronation dress. Coloured photography by Emil Rabending, 1867.

Above: The man Elisabeth cleverly used as a political 'instrument': Graf Gyula Andrássy (1823–1890).
Right: The actual creator of the 'compromise' with Hungary: Ferenc Deák (1803–1876).
Below: Coronation of Franz Joseph and Elisabeth to become Apostolic King and Queen of Hungary on June 8, 1867, manifestation of the new union with the Magyars.

Europe, of its most distinguished dynasty, and it became the triumph of Queen Erzebet – not Sissi. The Hungarians were thankful for her obvious dedication to the reaching of the Compromise – they idolised her far beyond her death. And she thanked them for this devotion by maintaining intense contact with the country and its people, even through friendships with Hungarian politicians, poets and scholars.

She also thanked her husband in a particular way. As a pledge for a renewed, solidified happiness she gave birth to another child in April 1868. Ten months after the coronation, Marie Valerie was born; she was raised by her mother as an independent and responsible-minded Hungarian.

After the coronation, the royal couple received the baroque hunting castle Gődöllő, east of Budapest as a present, for which Elisabeth had earlier shown interest. Franz Joseph, however, was unable to purchase it due to the financial burdens of the wars in 1859 and 1866.

The official coronation present of the Hungarian nation – 100,000 guilders – was dedicated to the widows and orphans of the soldiers who had fought in 1848/49 for Hungary's independence from Austria, a gesture that nobody dared ascribe to the proper, state-conscious emperor.

On the occasion of the coronation an impressive series of photos were taken, firstly in Budapest, later in Vienna of Elisabeth. They are masterfully arranged portraits of the woman who had just turned 30, whose beauty is coupled in an incomparable way with a soulful earnestness. A comparison with a portrait of her son Rudolf, when he was about 16 years old shows the deep affiliation of both these souls.

Below: Franz Joseph being sworn in as Apostolic King of Hungary on the Fischerbastei in Buda. Coloured lithograph by Vinzenz Katzler, 1867.

THE GLAMOUR AND TRAGEDY OF THE DYNASTY

At the beginning of the Seventies a worthy and politically promising marriage partner was sought for the growing children, and one of the first large family celebrations was held. Gisela became engaged to her Wittelsbach cousin Leopold in spring 1872, son of Luitpold of Bavaria, later Prince Regent. He was ten years older than her, had already distinguished himself in Prussia, and was a loyal hunting partner of the emperor. Elisabeth wasn't happy about this connection for her nephew belonged all too distinctly to the world of men, which she rejected. But she only had minimal influence over her eldest daughter, who had been taken away from her as a young child, then, however, she had made it possible herself through her escape from the Viennese court to influence the development of the girl.

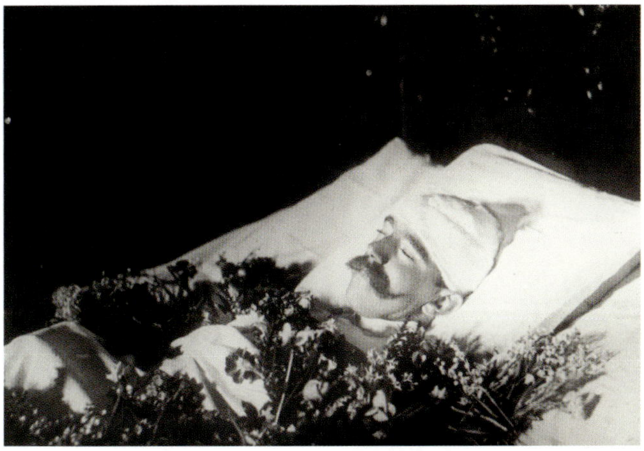

Through a genuine attachment and a growing satisfaction carried by the people, the imperial couple celebrated its silver wedding anniversary in 1879. The capital city and *Residenzstadt* Vienna had become a glittering city of architecture and arts due to its expansion, the Ringstrasse and the construction of numerous representative buildings. Since 1869, within about one decade, the court opera, the Musikverein building and the Academy of Fine Arts had been opened. Both court museums for the science and art collections of the imperial house were under construction as part of the planned Emperor's Forum – also the Burgtheater, today's parliament building and the Town Hall. The regulation of the Danube was completed and the new riverbed had been opened for shipping traffic in 1875.

In honour of the jubilant imperial couple the city of Vienna organised a parade with the Ringstrasse as its backdrop. The coordination was in the hands of the excellently appropriate painter Hans Makart, a favourite of the upper class. The imaginative paintings from the history of the House of Habsburg, its countries and the city of Vienna, as well as the varied 'living pictures' of artisans and artists of the 'Makart parade' ascquired legendary fame.

In 1881 Crown Prince Rudolf's engagement to Princess Stephanie of Belgium was announced. Her father was Leopold II, the infinitely rich King of Belgium and colonial ruler of the Congo, from the German princely house of Saxe-Coburg and Gotha. This family had become one of the most powerful of the century. The bride, hardly 16 years old, also came from an unhappy marriage, but in her innocence was more than willing to conduct a good marriage, which couldn't be said of the crown prince.

Following the failure of a strict military upbringing, the sensitive and intelligent boy was brought up by liberal teachers upon the insistence of Elisabeth, which lead to conflicts with his father and the court. Under the influence of a clique of officers of high nobility he was soon leading an unstable life, however without losing interest in the political system. As publisher of the comprehensive work "The Austro-Hungarian monarchy in words and pictures" he acquired lasting fame. The dedication to this publishing enterprise and also his interest in natural sci-

Above: Crown Prince Rudolf on his death bed. His suicide was publicly admitted after a brief hesitation. Photo, 1889.

Opposite page: One of the first large family celebrations: the engagement of Archduchess Gisela to Duke Leopold of Bavaria (standing on right). Left, Crown Prince Rudolf, front Archduchess Marie Valerie, sitting, the imperial couple. Coloured photograph based on an aquarelle by Emil von Hartitzsch.

Above: The imperial family in the year 1859. Standing from left: Franz Joseph, Ferdinand Maximilian (emperor-to-be of Mexico), his wife Charlotte, Ludwig Viktor and Karl Ludwig. In the first row from left: Elisabeth with Crown Prince Rudolf, daughter Gisela, her parents-in-law Sophie and Franz Karl. Photo by Ludwig Angerer.
Left: Sensitive and intelligent: Crown Prince Rudolf. Photo by Josef Albert, Munich, ca. 1873.
Opposite page: An idyll that never existed: Crown Prince Rudolf and Princess Stephanie of Belgium. Coloured photograph, Brussels, 1880.

ences – especially ornithology – and the 'hunting and research journeys' he undertook with the famous 'father of animals' Alfred Brehm for a time managed to uproot him from his environment. Under the protection of his anonymity he worked as a journalist for the liberal *Neues Wiener Tagblatt* (New Viennese Daily) run by his friend Moriz Szeps. As a critical intellect he fell out with all the institutions of the rulers – also with his father, who didn't assign him any duties.

For Stephanie the marriage to Rudolf was a great disappointment, and she didn't have any influence over him. The 'ideal', the way publicly distributed paintings from their first years of marriage showed, never existed. In fact these four people – Elisabeth and Franz Joseph, Stephanie and Rudolf – lived almost separate lives.

The only child of the Crown Prince couple was a girl, named after her grandmother Elisabeth. She had a long

and very active life ahead of her. After World War II she handed on some historically important portraits, which had been previously unknown, to the Austrian State. Among the memorable and significant paintings of her parents was also a portrait of her father as a youth, a painting by Heinrich Angeli.

On January 30, 1889 Crown Prince Rudolf committed suicide in the hunting castle Mayerling in the Wienerwald, and took the 17-year-old baroness Mary Vetsera with him. As appalling as Rudolf's suicide was for his parents – it was publicly admitted after a short, tormented hesitation – the murder of the girl was as insufferable. All information about the event was prohibited. Right up to the end of the monarchy it was the ultimate 'secret of Mayerling', which even today still gives rise to many suspicions.

The life and death of Crown Prince Rudolf are symptomatic of the situation in the Imperial Family and court society, but also for the political development of the Danube Monarchy. Its greatest problem was the foundation of an independent nation, the demand for which had arisen from all the peoples during Napoleon's time. "Each nation one state – the whole nation only one state" is how the motto ran, and the English and French media levied particularly aggressively for the Slavic people of the Danube Monarchy, blind to the fact that for a long time two large national states had existed (Great Britain and the USA), and that not all the French were united in one

Above: Living almost separate lives: Rudolf and Stephanie. Photo by C. Pietzner.
Below: Rudolf's suicide was a symptom of the monarchy's situation: The *Neue Freie Presse* announcing the crown prince's death, January 30, 1889.
Opposite page: Emperor Maximilian of Mexico's assassination on June 19, 1867, in Querétaro. Painting by Edouard Manet, 1867, Mannheim State Museum.

Neue
Freie Presse.
Abendblatt.

Nr. 8777. Wien, Mittwoch, den 30. Januar 1889.

† Kronprinz Rudolf.

Ein furchtbares, entsetzliches, niederschmetterndes Unglück hat sich ereignet. Kronprinz Rudolf, der Erbe des Thrones, die Hoffnung der Dynastie und des Reiches, ist todt!

In der Blüthe seiner Jahre, in strotzender Lebenskraft, das jugendliche Haupt voll Entwürfen für die Beglückung seines künftigen Reiches, für die Macht der Monarchie, für die Hebung von Kunst und Wissenschaft, hat einer jener tückischen, meuchlerischen Unfälle, welche der Neid der Götter zu entsenden pflegt, ihn auf unerklärliche Weise gefällt, seinem kaiserlichen Vater, seiner blühenden Gattin, seinem Kind, seinem Land, seinem Volke entrissen!

Der Schmerz, der Oesterreich-Ungarn getroffen hat, ist zu jäh, zu überwältigend zu riesengroß, um ihn auszudrücken; der Verlust, den wir erleiden, zu unermeßlich, um im ersten Augenblicke einer so furchtbaren Katastrophe sich seiner ganzen Größe bewußt zu werden. Das Schreckliche ist herniedergefahren wie der Blitz, der im Entstehen vernichtet. Die Thräne selbst versiegt von der Unermeßlichkeit solchen Schmerzes.

Soviel nur ist klar, daß mit dem heutigen Tage die Monarchie in ein Land der Klage und der Thränen verwandelt ist. Eine Hoffnung ist geknickt, auf deren Entfaltung Millionen Augen mit Sehnsucht geblickt haben; ein Leben hat geendet, das nichts als Liebe, Anmuth, Geist und Ritterlichkeit ausströmte; die unerforschliche Hand der Vorsehung hat ein schwarzes Gewölk vor eine Zukunft gehängt, die Allen goldig und verheißungsvoll erscheinen mußte, die diesen herrlichen Mann kannten oder von seinem, dem Vaterland, der Tugend, der Aufklärung gewidmeten Leben vernommen haben.

„Ein Meer von Licht möge von dieser Stadt ausströmen", war der Wunsch, den er einst seinem geliebten Wien widmete. Ein Meer von Thränen strömt nun von ihm selbst aus, da der erste Schmerz, den er seinem Lande und seinem kaiserlichen Vater bereitet hat, zugleich der größte sein mußte, der erdacht werden kann.

Gott tröste den Kaiser, das Reich, uns Alle, die wir ihn Alle verloren haben!

nation – for example, lived in the 'multinational state' Switzerland.
The emperor reacted to the existential problem of his state, continually using new approaches to find a solution by constantly changing the governments, which couldn't find any majorities in the Imperial Assembly. Elisabeth reacted by fleeing into a sentimental illusory world outside the monarchy, Rudolf by opposing his father and emperor as well as with critique of the politics of the ruling aristocratic society, the church and the nationalists, particularly the German nationals.
The monarchy's second largest problem was its independence from the German Empire under Prussian leadership. In the war that Germany fought against France in 1870/71, which led to the fall of Napoleon III and the conquest of the church state, Austria-Hungary remained neutral, though Franz Joseph didn't have any sympathies for this development. Austria remained Bismarck's obedient partner at the Berlin Congress, also during the solving of the problems that had developed through the Russian-Turkish war of 1877/78 in the Balkans.

Rudolf had found all this loathsome. Yet he had hoped for an improvement of the foreign political situation through the ascension to the throne of the liberal German Emperor Friedrich III in 1888. When the new emperor died after a few months he was followed by the hot-headed Wilhelm II, who was trapped in a militaristic world, who offended entire Europe with his megalomania. Rightly, Rudolf was afraid of the outbreak of a European war, which would destroy Austria-Hungary. For this reason Rudolf refused the close attachment of the Dual Alliance to Germany, but tried to establish a convergence with France. Neither his physical condition nor his character were up to the political acid test. But he didn't seek death due to political reasons. Rudolf was tense and overwrought to the highest degree, wasn't a sober, responsibly minded Habsburg-Lombardian. He was more a pathological-fanciful Wittelsbacher, like the mentally ill 'Fairy Tale King' Ludwig II of Bavaria and the mentally deranged Otto II – both his cousins – with a streak of contempt for mankind and disloyalty, which were totally foreign to Emperor Franz Joseph.

ELISABETH'S ODYSSEY

Their mutual suffering may have brought the emperor and the empress closer to each other, but also the consciousness of having to bear guilt for the tragic life of the crown prince. It had not only been Rudolf's father, who hid himself behind the facade of political correctness, but also his mother who had left her son alone for many years – though Rudolf had adored her and longed for her devotion. For this reason, she was blissfully ignorant at the time of Rudolf's suicide, and although she only ever thought about her beauty and independence and never tended to her country and its people, she only now became quasi homeless. But here we shouldn't overlook the fact that every year until her death she sojourned, often with her husband, in Budapest and Gődöllő, Ischl and also in Vienna.

For her cures she continued to go to Gastein, later also made one trip each to Karlovy Vary and Merano, and in the last two years of her life, to Bad Kissingen in Bavaria. However she only yearned for the Mediterranean, its islands and coasts and no longer England, for she had stopped riding. For physical fitness she now took hour-long walks, which extremely exhausted her company. Otherwise she now only travelled with a small entourage, usually only one court lady and a footman, which meant a decisive change.

On her first 'escape' to Madeira in1860 she was accompanied by 27 people; since 1874 on her sojourns in England and France, she had taken her expensive horses with her; had rail tracks laid for their transport and special stalls erected; building alterations, for example exercise rooms in the country residences, made in the country houses which she rented. In the spas she rented luxury hotel suites with up to 40 rooms. What was particularly contradictory was her love for the large – and anonymous – international hotels, which were ultimately decorated in the same style as the representative Villa Waldruh in the seclusion of the Lainzer Tiergarten in Vienna, whose impersonal atmosphere she tried to alter with several interventions. However the small castle only now referred to as the Hermesvilla had been designed by Franz Joseph's Ringstrasse architect Carl von Hasenauer and for that reason didn't suit her.

But soon after the Achilleion, which had been planned since 1888 and built according to 'her' tastes, was finished on the British island of Corfu, she lost her pleasure in it and its magnificent hanging gardens, "protected from unbidden gazes, fantastical, proud, sacred". She had been in Corfu for the first time as early as 1861, and her sojourn there was in keeping with her Wittelsbach love of Greece, especially since her cousin Otto was then still king of Greece. She had once mentioned to Franz Joseph that she saw the counrty as being her future home. In the year 1876 she visited Athens for the first time, in 1885 Troy and Egypt, and in both years, Corfu once more. Since 1886, also after the Achilleion had been completed, she combined the annual sojourns on the island with trips to the Mediterranean.

In November 1888, that is shortly before the death of the crown prince, she was in Greece and Asia Minor, one year later in Tunisia and on Malta, then again in Athens, Algeria, Sicily and Corsica; in 1891 she again travelled to Cairo

Above: Travelling as the purpose of life: Elisabeth at the window of the Albert atelier in Munich. Photo by Josef Albert, München 1865.
Opposite page: Elisabeth in Bad Kissingen, Bavaria, during a cure. Photo Atelier Neubauer, 1863.

from Corfu. Sissi spent the winter of 1892/93 travelling from island to island, visiting Seville and Barcelona. Finally she was on the French Riviera and for the first time in Territet on Lake Geneva. From there in April she travelled via Genoa and Naples to Corfu.

In order to be with her, often there was nothing left for the emperor to do but to follow his wife. From 1894 to1897 Elisabeth spent the winters at Cape Martin, where Empress Eugenie, widow of Napoleon III, inhabited a villa. There Elisabeth lived in the president suite of Hôtel du Cap Martin with 23 rooms. From here she visited the sophisticated locations on the Riviera, but mainly made excursions into the environs. After the often gruelling walks she had her weight monitored. Her Greek teacher often accompanied her on the trips.

Meetings with other crowned ladies who spent their time on the Riviera, mainly Empress Eugenie, but also Queen Victoria, were naturally unavoidable, although Elisabeth balked at every public appearance. For this reason she lapsed into the most absurd practices – she would leave the hotel through the back door and had her body guards disguised as postmen or street workers.

In the last two years of her life she only visited Vienna in passing. In December 1896 she travelled to Biarritz; in February and March 1897 she was in Cape Martin, then Territet, in Bad Kissingen, Ischl, Tyrol, in Budapest and Gődőllő, and at the turn of the year on the Riviera; in spring again in Territet, in Bad Kissingen, where she was visited by Franz Joseph, and in Bad Brückenau. Finally she travelled via Vienna to Ischl, where in July she saw the emperor for the last time. Thereafter she visited her siblings in Munich, took a spa in Bad Nauheim and then returned to Geneva Lake.

On September 9 she travelled over the lake to Geneva to spend the afternoon with Baroness Julie de Rothschild in Pregny and to admire her orchid garden. The empress spent the early evening in Geneva and stayed overnight in the famous Hotel Beau Rivage, where her apartment can still be visited. The next morning she ran some errands with her trusted court lady Countess Irma Sztáray, and, when at about half past one in the afternoon, she was about to board the steamer for the return trip, she was assassinated by an Italian anarchist with a needle file. It was September 10, 1898. An unfathomable senselessness, a deed

undertaken for its own sake, committed by a fatuous person who wanted to murder a head of state but didn't encounter one. Luigi Lucheni sent a restless woman, who may well have been tired of life, to her death. Sissi, however wasn't aware of this violent end because she didn't notice the injury, boarded the ship and broke down on board. She was taken back to the hotel unconscious, where she very quickly passed away.
Elisabeth's life was characterised by melancholy, as she herself once noted a few verses:

The big desire fades before the bigger one,
The heart is never satisfied,
And when happiness is found,
It is happiness no longer.

Right: Often having to do without the devotion of their mother: Elisabeth's daughters Gisela and Valerie in Bad Ischl. Photo, 1871.
Below: The "air is like a balm", wrote Elisabeth about Bad Kissingen: the Villa Mon Bijou. Photo, 1898.
Opposite page: Homeless: Elisabeth on Corfu. Posthumous portrait by Friedrich August von Kaulbach, after 1898. Hofmobiliendepot Vienna.

Above: Empress Elisabeth's return from a horse-back ride in Hyde Park for the Austrian Mission in London. Painting by Max Claude, 1874.
Left: Elisabeth's riding excursion in Biberach. Newspaper xylograph.
Right: Representation on horse-back: the imperial couple. Painting by Emil von Hartitzsch with mounted photographs of Emil Rabending and Ludwig Angerer, ca. 1867.

Above: Luxury in their 'rolling' hotel: the salon in Elisabeth's court salon carriage, built in 1873. Technical Museum, Vienna.
Left: The imperial yacht 'Miramar' was launched in 1872; its deck almost became Elisabeth's second home.

Opposite page
Above: The 'dying Achilles' in the Achilleion garden, a work by sculptor Ernst Herter from Berlin.
Below: "Fantastical, proud, sacred": the Achilleion on Corfu. Photo, ca. 1891.

Opposite page: Elisabeth's staple garment, her veil. Photo by Ludwig Angerer, 1862

Wiener

Tagblatt.

Demokratisches Organ.

Nr. 250. | Sonntag, den 11. September 1898. | 48. Jahrgang.

Die Kaiserin ermordet!

Genf, 10. September, 3 Uhr 40 Minuten Nachmittags. Kaiserin Elisabeth verließ um 12 Uhr 40 Minuten Mittags das Hotel Beaurivage, um sich nach dem Landungsplatze der Dampfer zu begeben.

Auf dem Wege dahin stürzte sich ein Individuum auf die Kaiserin und führte einen heftigen Stoß gegen dieselbe. Die Kaiserin fiel zu Boden, erhob sich jedoch wieder und erreichte den Dampfer, wo sie bald darauf in Ohnmacht fiel.

Der Kapitän des Schiffes wollte das Schiff nicht abgehen lassen, gab indes später über Bitten des kaiserlichen Gefolges das Zeichen zur Abfahrt. Das Schiff hielt jedoch, nachdem es den Hafen verlassen hatte, wieder an und kehrte zum Landungsplatze zurück. Die Kaiserin hatte das Bewußtsein nicht wiedererlangt und wurde auf einer rasch hergestellten Tragbahre nach dem Hotel Beaurivage gebracht.

Die Kleider der Kaiserin zeigten Blutflecken.

Der Thäter wurde festgenommen.

Right: News of Elisabeth's assassination threw the whole empire into profound mourning.
Below: The funeral: Sissi's coffin being carried in to the imperial crypt. Photo, September 17, 1898.

FRANZ JOSEPH AND THE LAST YEARS OF THE MONARCHY

It was often said that Franz Joseph had made a mistake in never apportioning his power, for example, to Crown Prince Rudolf, who by all means would have filled an independent sphere as Viceroy of Hungary or Bohemia. Now, with the emperor suddenly on his own after having lost so many family members through death, he was in even less of a position to distribute power.

When Archduke Carl Ludwig, the emperor's younger brother, died in 1896, his son Archduke Franz Ferdinand became heir to the throne. Yet Franz Joseph only assigned him military authority. His nephew's pronounced character, intolerant and prejudice prone, was in many ways contrary to the emperor's. Franz Ferdinand was fully convinced that the monarchy should be ruled in a very different way. He wanted to concede extensive independence to the Czechs and above all the Croats to contain the influence of the Hungarians.

Soon the archduke formed a type of shadow cabinet for 'X-Day', Franz Joseph's death, which the first in line to the throne never actually witnessed because he was assassinated in Sarajevo in 1914. Following the death of Empress Elisabeth, Archduchess Maria Theresa, Archduke Carl Ludwig's widow, became first lady of the court. Also the emperor's youngest daughter, Archduchess Marie Valerie, often played the role of home maker – mostly in Ischl.

Above: Power undelegated: Franz Joseph as the sovereign of the Order of the Golden Fleece. Painting by Sigismund Pollak, 1868.
Opposite page: Hunting companion King Eduard VII and Franz Joseph getting into a court carriage drawn by Lipizzans in Ischl. Photo court atelier Floeck, August 15, 1907.

Although Franz Joseph was in excellent health and rode horses until a ripe old age, life for him had become a burden. Death had also reaped its harvest amongst the emperor's generation of head-of-state peers.

The new generation of European rulers was either of nationalist bent or depended on the government, which paid homage to this ideology. In the year 1890 Emperor Wilhelm II fired his chancellor Prince of Bismarck. In 1894, Tsar Alexander III died, his successor Nicholas II would be the last tsar. Franz Joseph visited him in St. Petersburg in 1897, but wasn't able to prevent the imminent isolation of Austria-Hungary (and Germany), which threatened Russia's confederacies with France and England.

In the year 1900, King Umberto of Italy was assassinated. Victor Emanuel III acceded to the throne. Although connected to Austria-Hungary, Italy set its sights on tearing itself from the multinational Italian provinces. There were similar obscure circumstances in the relations to Great Britain, where, in January 1901, Queen Victoria died after 64 years of rule. Her successor Edward VII was a hunting companion of Franz Joseph's and, during a visit to Ischl in summer 1908 following a brief meeting with the tsar, attempted to dissolve the emperor's dependence to the German Empire – in vain.

Although Franz Joseph had suffered many indignities

through Prussia under Bismarck, he remained inflexible and immobile about his idea of being a 'German Prince'. The Prussian marshal's baton that Wilhelm II had given him in the year 1895 was probably more important to him than comparable distinctions that Edward VII afforded him. A striking event, which brought the 'German brotherhood in arms' into general consciousness, was the visit from a delegation of German princes to Vienna, when Franz Joseph's 60-year reign was being celebrated. Heading the delegation was Wilhelm II. All the princes wore uniforms; only the mayor from the hanseatic city of Hamburg wore antiquated black ceremonial garb.

Franz Joseph had himself once said that he indeed knew his multinational state was "an anomaly in the Europe of today," but nevertheless his approach was focused on the unity and indivisibility of the empire, and his position as ruler by the grace of God remained self-evident. In the process he was able to rely on the absolute admiration of the army and on a well-tested public service system. He was not without personal relations to the responsible figures of the State and military – and because he was aware of many particulars and kept a large number of names in his memory, he didn't forget any outstanding performances.

Austria-Hungary and Russia found themselves in opposition in the Balkans. In June 1903 Russia-supporting officers murdered their King Alexander I of Serbia, the son of Milan, who was allied with Franz Joseph, from the House of Obrenovic. The successor was the nationalistic Peter I from the House of Karadjordjevic, who was set on a coalition of all south-Slavic peoples who then lived in Austria-Hungary or the Ottoman Empire.

Austria-Hungary's position in Bosnia-Herzegovina was a thorn in the Serbs' side. The country that was subject to the Ottoman Empire's rule had been occupied by Austria since 1878. Thirty years later it was annexed, against

Below: Visits couldn't hinder the isolation of the Danube Monarchy: Tsarina Alexandra Feodorowna and Empress Elisabeth passing the gate of honour on Schwarzenbergplatz. Photo by Charles Scolik, 1896.
Opposite page: Father of the Nation and responsible for the integration of the empire: Franz Joseph I. Painting by Wilhelm Vita, 1893.

which the world powers first protested, however following Austria's agreement with Turkey, sanctioned the procedure. The country then underwent very positive development, thanks to huge investments in the areas of road and rail works, the health and school system and the establishment of an orderly administration.
Serbia's aspiration to be the leading power on the Balkan Peninsula was thus called into question; the brutal reaction couldn't be avoided. When successor to the throne Franz Ferdinand visited Sarajevo in summer 1914, he and his wife were assassinated on July 28 by young Serbian nationalists. Under the influence of the head of the military, who totally underestimated the risk of a huge war, one month later the emperor formulated the ultimatum to Serbia which triggered World War I because Russia immediately went to Serbia's aid and Germany to Austria-Hungary's. The war, which Karl Kraus described as "the last days of humanity," threw old Europe into ruins.
Franz Joseph returned from Ischl to Schönbrunn and ruled from there as a recluse. His successor, the last emperor, Carl, tried in vain to put an end to the flow of blood. Military leaders were unreasonable and remained so also after the defeat. The western powers, particularly France, were only interested in peace, which established the dissolution of the monarchy.
Emperor Franz Joseph died on November 21, 1916, in Schönbrunn Castle, where he had been born 86 years earlier. His body was laid to rest in the Emperor's crypt with the Capuchins. There he lies between the coffins of Elisabeth and his son Rudolf.

Farewell to an epoch: the funeral of Emperor Franz Joseph I on November 21, 1916. Coming from Heldenplatz, the hearse accompanied by body guards turns into the Ringstrasse. Photos from the Imperial and Royal court manufactury for photography, Vienna. Kunsthistorisches Museum, Department of Court Uniforms.

Photos and sources

MAGNO/Austrian Archives (AA): 2/3, 6/7, 9, 14, 18, 19 (above), 25, 29, 30, 35, 39, 41, 43, 44 (below), 46, 47, 50, 51 (above), 57 (below), 58, 61
IMAGNO/Schloss Schönbrunn Kultur und. Betriebsges. m.b.H.: 5, 12
IMAGNO/NB: 13, 16, 17, 26, 28, 34, 38, 42, 45, 48, 49, 51 (below), 52/53, 53 (below), 56, 60
IMAGNO/Dorotheum: 22
IMAGNO/Vienna library in the Town Hall: 27
Muzeum Narodowe, Cracow: 10
Archbishop's Cathedral and Diocesan Museum, Vienna: 11
Kunsthistorisches Museum Vienna: 19 (below), 20/21, 24, 33, 40 (below), 59, 62/63
Toni Anzenberger/Agentur Regina Maria Anzenberger: 31, 32, 36, 37
Wien Museum: 23, 40 (above left)
Austrian National Library, photo archive and portrait collection: 40 (above right), 44 (above)
Technical Museum Vienna: 54 (above)
Wladimir Aichelburg, K. u. K. Yachten. Vienna 1982. Reprint with friendly acknowledgement: 54 (below)
Auf Reisen mit Sisi. Pichler Verlag 2002: 55
Archive Pichler Verlag: 8, 52 (below), 57 (above)

The Author

Georg Kugler worked in the Kunsthistorisches Museum library from 1959 and in the Wagenburg at Schönbrunn, where he was director from 1973 to 2000. In 1990 he became assistant general director of the Kunsthistorisches Museum. Currently, Kugler is scientific director of the Lipizzan Musuem, and through numerous publications has become a leading authority on Viennese and Austrian cultural history. Included in his oeuvre is the major work *Die Lipizzaner der Spanischen Hofreitschule* (with W. Bihl), published in 2002. He has since published the guides *The Kunsthistorisches Museum Vienna* (2006) and *The Lipizzans* (2007).

ISBN 978-3-85431-446-2

www.pichlerverlag.at

Translation: Mag. Mý Huê McGowran

Book and cover design: Bruno Wegscheider
Production: Franz Hanns

Reproduction and image editing: Pixelstorm, Vienna
Printing and binding: Dimograf, Bielsko-Biała, Polen